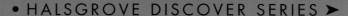

The Jurassic Coast
from the sea

Dorset and East Devon's World Heritage Site
through the lens of marine photographer

Steve Belasco

With a foreword by Chris Chibnall, creator of TV's *Broadchurch*

HALSGROVE

First published in Great Britain in 2022

Copyright © 2022 Steve Belasco

British Library Cataloguing-in-Publication Data
A CIP record for this title is available from the British Library

ISBN 978 0 85704 324 5

HALSGROVE
Halsgrove House,
Ryelands Business Park,
Bagley Road, Wellington, Somerset TA21 9PZ
Tel: 01823 653777   Fax: 01823 216796
email: sales@halsgrove.com

Part of the Halsgrove group of companies
Information on all Halsgrove titles is available at:
www.halsgrove.com

Printed and bound by Parksons Graphics, India

Contents

Foreword

NEW YEAR, 2004. Lyme Regis. On a last-minute booking, we'd escaped our 10th floor London flat with our three-month-old firstborn son, and rented a pink thatched cottage on the front in Lyme Regis, overlooking the sea.

I'd never been to Dorset before. We knew no-one in this part of the world.

Within six months we'd moved here. Within six years, I'd started to think about writing a television series set here. That's what this coastline does to you. That show, *Broadchurch*, was a love letter to this landscape.

It was only while filming *Broadchurch* that I first saw the Jurassic Coast from the sea. It changes your perspective entirely, making you re-evaluate the shapes and scale and wonder.

It's a rare privilege and wonderful point of view, showcased by Steve's gorgeous photography. I'm grateful he's sharing it with the rest of us, in this beautiful book.

Chris Chibnall

Acknowledgements

Thanks so much to:
My (usually) patient wife Josie and sons Louis and Tristan
Drama genius Chris Chibnall (and Maddy)
My good friends at Portland Marina
The ever-helpful harbourmaster, pilots and staff at Portland Port
The harbourmasters at Lyme Regis and Exmouth for their kindness
The RNLI and National Coastwatch Institution for being there
Our inshore fishermen for putting up with me pointing my lens
at them as they go about their tough jobs
Sylvia Webster and Neil Roberts for their photos of me
The experts in their fields, especially Dr Ian West, Stuart Morris and Peter Bruce
The Jurassic Coast Trust team, especially Alex and Guy, and my fellow ambassadors
Dan Stuttle for looking after the boat
The proud and supportive islanders of Portland
The friendly crew at The Boat That Rocks
And of course, Steven Pugsley, Sharon O'Inn, Lorraine Inglis and the team at Halsgrove

Introduction

THIS BOOK OF PHOTOGRAPHS is all about the Jurassic Coast in the twenty-first century.

The coast is constantly changing, evolving and eroding, as it has done for millions of years, and we humans are merely the creatures privileged to be enjoying it for the time being.

It's a very different animal to what it was 200 million years BC but that, of course, is a major part of its rollercoasting charm.

I've had the good fortune of sailing up and down these waters for more than twenty-five years and I'm still stunned by the variety of vistas. There is beauty and austerity, serenity and violence.

Capturing the natural and human activity in these waters has been a wonderful experience, and whatever is happening, it always happens with this sublime Jurassic

Portland Bill.

(also Cretaceous and Triassic) backdrop. And I continually wonder at the unique quality of light that seems to exist offshore.

I capture nearly all of my images aboard my motorboat *Strange Weather*. (Here I must confess I've sneaked just a couple of 'shoreside' images into this book.) Although I'm usually on my own – except when my faithful seadog Zelda accompanies me – it's worth remembering that there can be great joy in being alone; the term is 'solitude'. Loneliness, on the other hand, is the misery of being alone; and it's only on a bleak and grey winter's afternoon that I may feel a little bit of the latter. But only a bit. There's always some maritime activity or other going on, or some creature up to something to focus my lens or thoughts upon.

And, truthfully, I can only once remember spending more than a couple of hours afloat without seeing another boat at all.

My reason for this labour of love is to present the Jurassic Coast of Dorset and East Devon to our society as widely as possible. I'm incredibly proud of my adopted home and want as many people as possible to appreciate it and, ultimately, to visit and enjoy.

It's the only natural site in England that has been awarded World Heritage status by UNESCO but, perhaps surprising to some, that's not because of its beauty but 'for its contribution to Earth science'.

I'm also a volunteer ambassador for the Jurassic Coast Trust, the charity that manages, teaches and promotes the coastline to the wider world. There are scientists, professors and experts of almost every description in the trust, and a huge amount has been and is being written and published about the geology, history, fauna and of course, fossils.

So my mission has been to photograph and present the Jurassic Coast and its waters, from sea level, as it is today – including how we humans use, enjoy, modify and interfere with it (with a glance at the towns that bookend the stretch).

We're amidst a continually-developing process and the area is as active now as at any other time in its long history (although geologically, it's rather less brisk!)

Until relatively recently there have only been drawings and maps imagining how it all used to look. But many years down the line our descendants will have photographic, (probably holographic and who knows what else), records of the now to examine and enjoy.

I do hope this book will make a small contribution to that future knowledge.

1 The East End

THE JURASSIC COAST is bookended by the port towns of Poole in the east and Exmouth in the west.

Poole has been in Dorset for centuries but its close neighbour Bournemouth only stepped over the county boundary, from Hampshire, in the local government reorganisation of 1974.

Poole boasts one of the world's largest natural harbours, at 14 square miles. But it's very shallow, with an average depth of just 48 centimetres!

Nonetheless, the deeper areas are extremely busy, with a prosperous freight and ferry port, a Royal Marines base, thousands of boating enthusiasts and just about the full gamut of water sports, not to mention an abundance of wildlife.

The harbour also boasts the headquarters of the RNLI, a thriving fishing fleet and luxury yacht builders as well as six nature reserves!

Settlements have been found that pre-date Roman times and the harbour is home to Wytch Farm, the largest onshore oil field in western Europe, with its workings well-hidden in a forest on its southern shores.

There are inevitably conflicts of interest between the commercial, recreational, military and environmental fraternities. But it all seems to be admirably managed by the Poole Harbour Commissioners, a trust which oversees the various interests so they can operate in harmony to ensure the long-term sustainability of the harbour.

Heading out of the narrow harbour entrance we pass the Cote d'Azur of the south coast, the Sandbanks Peninsula, one of the most expensive real estate locations on the planet and home to its share of resident celebrities.

But the biggest celebrity of all, the Jurassic Coast, starts its 96-mile journey from east to west just across at Studland Bay where Cretaceous chalk dominates, reminiscent of Dover's white cliffs. This is the 'young' end of the Jurassic Coast, at around 55 million years, and our journey to the west takes us back in time through almost 200 million more!

Highly popular with boaters for its gentle, sheltered beauty – except when there's east in the wind – Studland was used for D-Day landing rehearsals and testing due to its similarity to some Normandy beaches. It is well protected from the prevailing westerly winds by the bulk of Ballard Down and the Handfast Peninsula.

On one memorable April day in 1944, Winston Churchill, General Eisenhower, King George VI, Admiral Mountbatten and Field Marshall Montgomery were all gathered within the thick concrete walls of the sinister Fort Henry to watch live weapons practise.

The fort was the largest and possibly the most important observation post in the British Isles.

Studland Bay is bordered to the west by golden, gentle beaches and to the south by the chalky corrugated cliffs known as The Yards and the more well-known Old Harry Rocks.

Old Harry is thought to be named after the notorious but highly-successful local pirate, or privateer, Harry Paye who would sneak to and fro out of Poole, passing the eponymous stack on his way to attacking the French or Spanish merchantmen that passed by, as well as when setting off to raid foreign coastal settlements.

Another reason could be that Henry VIII built a fort, Studland Castle, here which has long since disappeared into the sea.

A third possibility has it that the devil himself once slept on the rocks.

Next to Old Harry, who stands 61 feet tall, is the rather diminutive stump known as Old Harry's Wife. She's just a shadow of her former self after the once much-taller stack collapsed in a storm. But erosion could well bring Harry down to nearer her size before too long.

Keeping the vertical white wall of the Handfast Peninsula, topped by Ballard Down, to the right, means passing more stacks, called The Pinnacles, before rounding Ballard Point into Swanage Bay.

A favourite with thousands of holidaymakers, the safe, sandy beaches of Swanage have attracted many famous visitors, with Noddy creator and prolific children's author Enid Blyton perhaps the most well-known resident.

Swanage was originally a fishing village and small port, but found real fortune in Victorian times exporting the much-prized Purbeck stone, quarried nearby, by sea to London and elsewhere and it soon became a popular upmarket resort for the wealthy of the time.

Previous page: The small peninsula of Sandbanks, which crosses the mouth of Poole Harbour, is one of the most expensive places to live on the planet. Real estate here is said to boast the fourth highest land value in the world with only London, Manhattan and Tokyo cited as costing more.

Inset: Just inside the harbour lies Brownsea Island with its elegant castle.

Facing out across Studland Bay is the sinister concrete slab of Fort Henry at Redend Point. It is from this lookout position, some 90 feet long with 3-feet thick walls, that Winston Churchill, General Eisenhower, King George VI, Admiral Mountbatten and Field Marshall Montgomery watched rehearsals for the D-Day landings in 1944.

It's easy to see why beautiful Redend Point on the western side of Studland Bay is so called. The striking colouring of the usually brown and yellow sandstone is formed by seepage caused by iron oxidation. Early morning sunrise, as pictured here, is the best time to appreciate the area which, of course, is east facing.

The shallow chalk bays and cliffs to the south west of Studland Bay are known locally as *The Yards (promonteries)* and lead on to Old Harry Rocks just to the south.

Sheltered Studland is very popular with boaters and includes a voluntary no-anchor zone to protect some of the important marine life here. This includes seagrass meadows which provide a home for undulate rays and pipefish and a breeding ground for cuttlefish and both species of our protected native seahorses.

Left: *The chalk at the Handfast Peninsula is gradually being eroded away to create caves and arches. This is No-Man's-Land.*

Right: *Old Harry and his much-diminished wife. She was originally much taller and looks to me like she's now facing away, sulking, from poor Harry...*

A beautiful sunset at Handfast Point. Old Harry's diminutive wife can be seen at far right.

Opposite page, top: *The Handfast Peninsula can be quite dazzling in bright sunshine.*
Bottom: *A local sailing club's evening race passes Old Harry Rocks. In the distamce are Swanage and Durlston Head.*

The Cretaceous chalk of the Handfast Peninsula glows warmly at sunrise.

Ballard Point, beneath grassy Ballard Down, marks the eastern end of Swanage Bay.

The handsome resort of Swanage, which was once a tiny fishing village, came to prominence in Victorian times as the chief exporter of Purbeck stone, quarried nearby, and subsequently as a posh holiday destination for the wealthy.

Opposite page, top: *Peveril Point. The National Coastwatch Institute lookout point can be seen as a trip boat passes heading in to Swanage.* Bottom: *The Peveril Ledge forms a notorious race off Peveril Point at the southern tip of Swanage Bay when a strong tide is running. The prominent red buoy indicates how far out the ledge extends, even though it is still not quite at the outmost point.*

2 A Coastful of Quarries

THE SEVEN-MILE STRETCH of coastline from Swanage as far as mighty St Aldhelm's Head has been largely shaped by man. Purbeck limestone was and is much sought after and was hand-hewn for centuries; the Romans coveted the beautiful Purbeck marble which they used for their villas and tombs and were probably the first to quarry in significant quantities here.

Technically it isn't true marble because it's not metamorphic, but it polishes up and looks just as good.

Purbeck marble was revered enough to be used in cathedrals including Exeter, Ely, Norwich, Chichester, Salisbury, Lincoln, Southwark and Canterbury and in Westminster Abbey.

Christopher Wren later relied heavily on the hard-wearing and durable Purbeck and Portland stone – laid down in the younger Jurassic period, around 135 to 150 million years ago – when rebuilding London after the great fire of 1666.

As the most practical way of transporting the heavy slabs was by sea it was natural that the coast was the focal point for the quarrymen, who gave their places of work wonderfully-evocative names like Dancing Ledge, Winspit, Seacombe and Tilly Whim.

Blocks were lowered by wooden cranes, or derricks, onto small barges called lighters which then transported them offshore to larger ships.

It is difficult to imagine how skilfully the wooden boats were navigated right alongside the unforgiving rock, with no engines and at the mercy of the wind and tide, though there were inevitably plenty of casualties.

One of Dorset's two proper lighthouses is at Anvil Point, alongside the old Tilly Whim quarry.

There are no longer any working quarries on the coast here, but their legacy provides a rugged and fascinating insight into the past for the thousands of visitors and locals who make their way to soak up the ambience and explore here every year; there is still much evidence of the activity that peaked in the eighteenth and nineteenth centuries.

The unusual landscape has attracted a variety of media production teams. Winspit quarry became the Dalek's home planet Skaro for episodes of *Doctor Who*, and the BBC's sci-fi people even returned later for an episode of *Blake's 7*.

St Aldhelm's Head has a powerful tidal race, rather like a slightly smaller version of that at Portland Bill, and the seas here can be very rough. There are many shipwrecks in the area.

The head, usually now referred to as St Alban's Head, is quite imposing when viewed from

Previous page: *A yacht sails past Anvil Point and Tilly Whim caves.*

Left: *Durlston Bay. The shallow bay is largely unprotected and there is considerable cliff recession in the area. It is designated an area of high ecological and geological importance, but much of the cliffs' evolution is more visible from seaward than ashore. Here there is interesting rock strata exposed – dotted amongst the verdant growth – which is not easily seen from the shore.*

Opposite page: *At the southern end of Durlston Bay lies bulbous Durlston Head. The headland forms a part of the eponymous country park and national nature reserve which amounts to 320 acres of countryside carefully managed by Dorset County Council. There is an amazing diversity of flora and fauna amongst the nationally-important wildlife habitats and sea-cliffs. The eminent Victorian George Burt left a variety of artefacts here, including Durlston Castle, top right, and the Great Globe – just visible in the centre of the photo – carved from 40 tonnes of Portland limestone. They are all linked by scenic cliff-top paths and well worth a visit, though not at all accessible by sea!*

the sea. It rises to 108 metres – much higher than Portland Bill – and passing it close by in a small boat is in some ways more unsettling.

The headland was so-named after the Bishop of Sherborne, later revered as Saint Aldhelm, who had apparently stopped here en route to Rome for a meeting with Pope Sergius.

The tiny Norman St Aldhelm's Chapel at the top is square and believed to have formerly served as a lookout before taking on its religious role.

There's also an interesting memorial atop the cliff which celebrates the part the area played in Radar research during the last war. It is said to have been crucial to the winning of the war and to modern communications. Both the chapel and memorial can only just be seen with a keen eye from sea level, though they are visited frequently by land.

Left: *Also forming part of Durlston Country Park is Anvil Point lighthouse and Tilly Whim caves. The lighthouse is one of the dumpiest in the country, at just 12 metres high, though the light itself sits 45 metres above sea level. It was formally opened in 1881 by Neville Chamberlain's father, the then Minister of Transport.*

The caves, formed of three former quarries worked predominently in the eighteenth century, are now closed to the public for safety reasons. The quarrymen used an early type of crane called a 'whim' and George Tilly was a well-known local character, perhaps suggesting the origins of the name...

Below: *The low, 4-mile stretch of Purbeck coastline between Anvil Point and St Aldhelm's Head is dotted with quarries and mysterious nooks, coves and caves. These anglers are fishing off the sinister recess of Blacker's Hole.*

Above: *Among the cliffs beneath Anvil Point lighthouse lies the enclosed and atmospheric climbing spot known as Black Zawn. Experienced climbers describe it as requiring an abseil approach and 'a degree of commitment' as can be seen from this photo!*

Left: *Keen coasteerers can be found even on a chilly and uninviting October day.*

Much of the Jurassic Coast can only be truly appreciated by being viewed from seaward. This pretty spot is Green Point, just a few metres – but virtually unseen – from its famous neighbour, Dancing Ledge. The water trickling over the edge which causes the algal greenery is the result of a geological fault.

Dancing Ledge, probably the best-known former Purbeck coastal quarry. There is continuing debate over the origin of the name, one suggestion being that when the waves undulate over the lower ledge at certain stages of tide, it appears to be dancing. Others say it was once described as being as big and flat as a dance floor and yet others that it could be a derivation of 'dark spring ledge'. Whichever it is, the ledge drops off steeply enough for small ships to have come alongside in the past and transported stone directly from its source. A good deal of Ramsgate Harbour in Kent was constructed with stone sailed directly from here in the seventeenth and eighteenth centuries.

Purbeck's coastal quarries feature arrays of man-made caves, or galleries, from whence the stone was cut and extracted. After open-cast quarrying had removed much of the easily-accessible building stone, drift-mining techniques were used to work horizontally into the cliffs. The galleries, of up to 60 metres deep, were cut and quarrymen would either shore up the roof by leaving some of the rock in situ or by building up stone pillars. Dozens of the angular openings are still visible, particularly from offshore.

Winspit was a very large coastal quarry which is now a fascinating and atmospheric destination for walkers and picnickers. It is bordered by two hills, West Man and East Man. Easily-quarried, highly-fractured limestone made it a particularly productive site which has left many galleries and workings, some of which have been used as mysterious television and movie locations.

Inland from Winspit is the Purbeck village of Worth Matravers and it's easy to see where the stone used to build the village came from!

Above: *Wildlife is, of course, abundant along this undisturbed stretch of coast; here a pair of busy guillemots are captured under St Aldhelm's Head.*

Right: *This strange natural feature near St Aldhelm's Head, is called, rather unsurprisingly, a 'topple' by geologists.*

St Aldhelm's Head in late afternoon. The headland is rightly feared by mariners in bad weather and many vessels have come to grief in the attendant race. Although described as a lesser version of Portland Bill, it can be just as dangerous and, at 108 metres high it towers above its more notorious cousin.

Houns-tout and Egmont Point with Rope Lake Head in the distance. Once around the 'corner' of St Aldhelm's Head, dark shale is revealed. This oil shale, or blackstone, consists of up to 70 per cent organic matter which makes it one of the highest by proportion in the world. There was much oil shale mining at Kimmeridge in the past and the derived gas was apparently used to light Wareham's street lights in 1848.

Sir William Clavell used it as fuel for his explorations into the manufacture of salt and glass in the seventeenth century.

3 Bleak and Beautiful

THE STRETCH FROM St Aldhelm's Head up to White Nothe and the start of Weymouth Bay is a mixture of remote shorelines and awkward-to-access cliffs interspersed with popular visitor destinations. Between spots like Chapman's Pool, Brandy Bay and the massive chalk headland of White Nothe, which can all be hard work to get to, lie visitor hotspots like Kimmeridge Bay, Lulworth Cove and Durdle Door.

They all present interesting faces when viewed from offshore and much of the area simply cannot be seen or appreciated properly from land.

Several of these locations are easier to visit by sea than by land, although there are plenty of hazards for the unwary boater. The infamous Kimmeridge Ledges extend several miles offshore along here and have claimed many ships. A series of reefs perpendicular to the coast give depths of water that vary steeply between a metre and perhaps 10 metres. Accurate pilotage is needed to get a boat in close to places like Egmont Bight, Clavell's Hard and Rope Lake Head.

From the towering coastal cliffs of St Aldhelm's Head, Emmetts Hill and Egmont Point, the coastline drops down to a stretch of dark, low cliffs for several miles to Kimmeridge Bay.

This coastline is largely oil-rich shale, which sometimes gives the water a dark, slightly menacing hue.

In the past, particularly the seventeenth century, the shale was used to produce alum and for other industrial purposes. Principal in these was local landowner Sir William Clavell, who has given his name to the once-busy landing point of Clavell's Hard and, indirectly, the famous Clavell Tower.

Some of the seams were rich enough in oil to burn domestically like coal, and there were a succession of short-lived enterprises. But these failed, mainly due to the shale's high sulphur content, making most of it unsuitable for domestic use particularly because of the foul stench... the sulphur could not be removed with the technology available at the time.

Indeed a few barrels of oil are still being extracted from Kimmeridge Bay by a lonely 'nodding donkey' pump, which is only just commercially viable now.

While much of this coastline does look grim and inhospitable in bad weather – and there are really no ports of refuge for the mariner if an onshore wind pipes up – it's all a delight when the weather is calm and the sun comes out.

Kimmeridge Bay is within the Purbeck Marine Wildlife Reserve and boasts the best rockpooling and snorkelling in Dorset. It is very popular with visitors and there is a marine centre and a new fossil museum.

Passing Brandy Bay and the mighty Gad Cliff, everything brightens up as chalk reappears at beautiful Worbarrow after heading inland for a few miles.

So, having cruised past the Cretaceous chalk of Old Harry and the older Jurassic limestone of the Purbeck Peninsula, we're back looking at younger Cretaceous chalk again! These anomalies are all part and parcel of what makes the Jurassic Coast unique in the world.

The eastern end, the actual Worbarrow Bay, is bookended by Worbarrow Tout and the old hill fort of Flowers Barrow which is rapidly collapsing into the sea.

Worbarrow fronts the Army's tank firing practice ranges at Lulworth and the land and sea areas here are often closed to the public for safety reasons.

From towering Bindon Hill, backing Mupe Bay at the western end of Worbarrow, the coast is now mostly chalk as far as the precipitous headland of White Nothe – which marks the start of Weymouth Bay – interspersed with rocky delights such as Lulworth Cove, Dungy Head and Durdle Door; probably the most photographed and well-known spot in Dorset.

Black with white. The dark shale of Rope Lake Head contrasts with the chalk of distant Bindon Hill.

A motor yacht anchored in Rope Lake Hole near Kimmeridge. The low oil shale cliffs of 'Kimmeridge coal' here are a not unpleasant hue when the sun shines, although they can look bleak and uninviting on a grey day. They are lightened up by white layers at the joints. The water is usually dark though.

Kimmeridge Bay from the south-west. Clavell's Tower, sitting above Hen Cliff, is picked out by the sunlight. It was built as an observatory and folly around 1830 by John Clavell-Richards, who had inherited the Smedmore estate in 1817. Part of Smedmore House, originally built by Sir William Clavell in the early seventeenth century, can just be seen, centre, amongst the trees.

Kimmeridge Bay, overlooked by Clavell's Tower, is a Mecca for watersports enthusiasts.

Shale workers' cottages at Kimmeridge. Note the west to east downward tilt of the rock layers, which is noticeable in most of these images of the Jurassic Coast.

Broad Bench, on the western side of Kimmeridge Bay. Beyond it is the towering Gad Cliff.

A yacht anchored in Worbarrow Bay. The soft, sandy Wealden cliffs behind show the marl, lignite and sandstone that produce the beautiful pinks.

Left: *Due to erosion, the large iron-age hill fort Flowers Barrow is rapidly collapsing. This location is the western end of the ridge that first started at Ballard Down, north of Swanage. The sunlight picks out some of the more recent land movements.*

Below: *A yacht passes Arish Mell gap at the centre of Worbarrow Bay. Lulworth Castle can be seen peeping out from behind the trees. This area is often closed to the public as it forms part of the Army's Lulworth gunnery ranges.*

The tall ship Earl of Pembroke *sails along the western end of the Purbeck coastline including Bats Head, Hambury Tout, Lulworth Cove and Bindon Hill.*
Right, above: *Pretty Lulworth Cove is hugely popular all year round, and has attracted many famous names such as Jane Austen, James Whistler, Bertrand Russell and poets John Keats and Rupert Brooke. Movie star Brad Pitt even shot scenes for his zombie movie* World War Z *here!*
Below: *A squadron of Canada geese swoops in low towards Dungy Head like the Dambusters heading for the Ruhr.*

A lone climber clings, limpet-like, to the arch of Durdle Door.

Opposite page: *Probably Dorset's most famous landmark, Durdle Door, at sunrise on midwinter's day. The natural limestone arch was created by the sea finally wearing through the vertical limestone which was uplifted after Africa and Europe collided, beginning 24 million years ago. This is the same tectonic activity that created the Alps!*

I am regularly surprised and delighted by the sights that greet me. Here, while passing Bull Rock one gentle summer's evening, a pair of 'mermaids' sprang up from nowhere! Bat's Head and White Nothe are in the distance.

Opposite: *A 'Wolf Moon' rises behind Durdle Door on a January evening.*

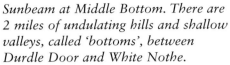

Sunbeam at Middle Bottom. There are 2 miles of undulating hills and shallow valleys, called 'bottoms', between Durdle Door and White Nothe.

Grazing sheep can be seen dotted about like dandruff on Chaldon Down. The green and white diagonal striations are caused by vegetation growing atop old stepped chalk slips. The vertical cliff, far left, is called Fountain Rock.

Opposite page: White Nothe. The imposing, 160-metre-high chalk headland marks the border between the districts of Purbeck and West Dorset and forms the eastern end of Weymouth Bay. Fresh chalk falls can be seen in this image. A steep, zig-zag path up the cliff was alluded to as the smugglers' path in J. Mead Faulkner's famous novel Moonfleet.

Bats Head, Lone Beach and Middle Bottom photographed from off Angel Bay. Some stretches of the coast here are only accessible by boat and even that can involve tricky pilotage. St Aldhelm's Head, 12 miles distant, can just be seen extreme right.

4 A Jurassic Borough

THE SEASIDE BOROUGH of Weymouth and Portland (though technically no longer a borough) needs little introduction. Hugely popular with tourists, day visitors and fans of all types of water sports, the municipality sits geographically midway along the Jurassic Coast.

Weymouth's gentle beaches and pretty harbour, at the mouth of the River Wey, combined with the Isle of Portland's plunging cliffs, huge harbour and crystal clear waters, provide a magnet for families, sailors, climbers, divers, anglers and wildlife lovers.

Weymouth (then called Melcombe Regis), came to fame when King George III started to visit after being recommended by his physicians to take the air and to the water for his ailing health.

From 1789 the king spent 14 summer holidays here and used a special bathing machine to enter the sea, away from too many prying eyes. His entourage and court followers soon established the town as one of the country's first modern seaside destinations. And the splendid Georgian Esplanade is still stunning to look at from offshore. A huge image of George astride his horse is carved into a chalk hillside near Osmington.

I think of Portland as the island that built London for its eponymous stone appears almost everywhere in the capital.

How about Buckingham Palace, St Paul's Cathedral, Bank of England, London Bridge, the Tower of London, the British Museum, National Gallery and The Cenotaph for starters? Further afield are many more including a host of buildings in Washington DC and New York's famous United Nations building.

Incidentally, the limestone-loving architect Sir Christopher Wren was once the MP for Weymouth and Melcombe Regis, albeit for a rather short time.

Mention must also be made of Portland Bill. Originally 'Beel', meaning beak, the protuberance of Portland doesn't stop at the sea's edge but continues southwards out into the Channel for some miles as a huge underwater ledge.

This ledge has deep, steep sides and is thought to harbour canyons and giant caves that could swallow St Paul's Cathedral.

In bad weather this dangerous area is notorious for its extremely confused and violent tidal races and shallow Shambles Bank and is understandably the most feared headland on the south coast for mariners.

Previous page: *Gravity-defying sheep graze on the cliffs near Ringstead in Weymouth Bay. A layer of the dark oil and gas shale last seen at Kimmeridge makes a reappearance here thanks to landslips in Ringstead Bay. A section, still known as Burning Cliff, smouldered here for several years from 1826.*

One of several campsites that accommodate the thousands of visitors each year.

Opposite page: *Sailing is, of course, part and parcel of Weymouth and Portland and local waters are regarded as some of the finest in Europe. It's a rare day when there is no sailing activity at all and it's no coincidence that these waters were chosen to host the sailing events of the 2012 Olympic Games, above. The various sailing clubs hold race series and regattas throughout the year and the summer evening series are always particularly popular. Weymouth's superb Georgian seafront provides a fine backdrop whatever the level of racing that is taking place.*

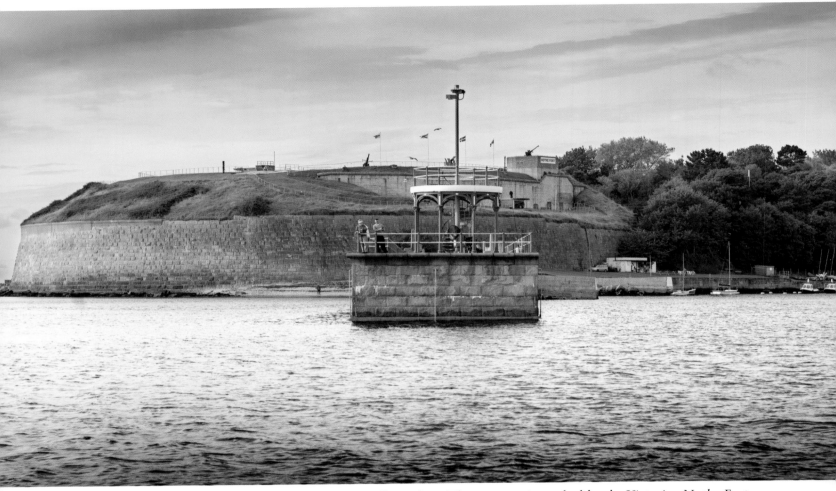

Weymouth's Harbour provides refuge for vessels in all weathers. The entrance is marked by the Victorian Nothe Fort, built between 1860 and 1872 to protect Portland Harbour which by then was a very important strategic base for the Royal Navy. The guns also covered the approaches to Weymouth Harbour. It was also an important defence in the Second World War for British and US troops passing through and remains one of the best preserved of its kind in the country. It's a popular tourist attraction, now maintained by Weymouth Civic Society.

Perpendicular to the fort, the southern arm of the harbour entrance, known as the Stone Pier, is popular with anglers, allowing them to cast well offshore.

Weymouth's busy inner harbour boasts two marinas and is accessible to yachts via the lifting Town Bridge. The sixth bridge built since 1597 to unite the formerly separate towns of Weymouth and Melcombe Regis, the electrically-operated bascule bridge was opened in 1930 by The Duke of York, later King George VI. It usually lifts every two hours during daytime.

Weymouth's quayside is a busy and colourful place even well outside the main season. The handsome orange and white Georgian building at left was the headquarters of Portland Coastguard until government cuts took the safety administration of these busy waters nearly 60 miles away to Lee-on-the-Solent in Hampshire in 2014.

Midweek evening yacht racing is very popular in Weymouth Bay. The distant hilltop monument on Black Down honours Sir Thomas Masterman Hardy, Admiral Lord Nelson's flag captain, who lived nearby.

Opposite: Big ships frequently visit Weymouth Bay. Here, a bottlenose dolphin breaches right under the bow of a giant tanker.

THE JURASSIC COAST FROM THE SEA

Of course, the marine industry plays a major part in the waters of the Jurassic Coast and is the largest source of income for many businesses here. Weymouth Bay is a popular anchorage for ships of all sizes, whether to shelter from a period of of nasty westerly weather or for bunkering (refuelling) or crew changes.

Portland Port is the harbour authority which administers the area and huge tankers often visit. VK Eddie is nearly 160,000 tonnes GRT and is one of the largest ever to come into the bay. She is pictured here being refuelled – rather like the tiny bird feeding the cuckoo in her nest – by the Portland Bunkers UK ship Fredericia, no tiddler herself at more than 2000 tonnes!

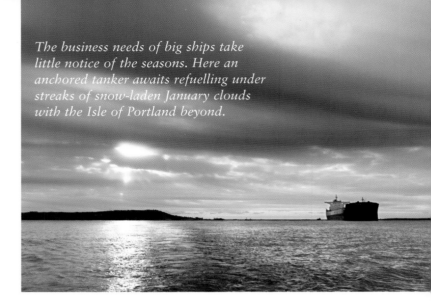

The business needs of big ships take little notice of the seasons. Here an anchored tanker awaits refuelling under streaks of snow-laden January clouds with the Isle of Portland beyond.

The fishing industry is also an integral part of Jurassic Coast life, with all the coastal towns boasting thriving fleets. Although the counties' lucky residents are usually spoilt for choice when it comes to fresh seafood, business dictates that much of it is shipped speedily away to some of Britain's, and indeed Europe's, swankiest restaurants and markets.

The Coronavirus Pandemic of 2020 and 2021 meant that most of the world's fleet of cruise ships had to 'hibernate' for long periods. Several spent many months anchored in Weymouth Bay including, above, Cunard's Queen Mary 2 *and* Queen Victoria.

Opposite: The anchored cruise ships attracted lots of small fish which in turn persuaded several dolphins to take up residence in the area, rather than just passing through!

Above: *Portland's stone industry is, of course, legendary and is what made the island famous across the world. For centuries the stone was shipped by sea, being lowered from the cliff tops into boats or ships, but the advent of railways and then better roads eventually killed off the most logical mode of transport. But all along the eastern and southern coast of the island are reminders of those days, including piles of cut slabs that were ready to go and the famous Portland cranes, very few of which remain. Freshwater Bay, here, is overlooked by the imposing Young Offenders Institution.*
Below: *Broad Ope was once a hive of stone-loading activity and one of its cranes remains.*

Opposite: *Church Ope Cove and Rufus Castle, Portland. The beautiful cove is understandably popular with islanders, some of whom have their own beach huts here, but it can be a bit of an effort to get to. Towering above are the remains of Rufus Castle, known locally as Bow and Arrow Castle. The blockhouse was built by Richard, Duke of York, in the fifteenth century, but is thought to be on the site of a much earlier, Norman, building built for William II.*

Times change and what was once a stone loading site called Sandholes becomes a popular spot for the relatively new sport of coasteering, which combines swimming with low-level rock climbing. Visitors come from far and wide to make the most of these wonderful locations, again bolstering the local economy – the evolving Jurassic Coast continues to provide in one way or another.

Similarly, wildlife uses the crags and crevices for protection. This is a group of guillemots.

Opposite page: *Portland Bill at sunset. The headland on the south coast most feared by mariners is pretty tame in gentle weather but ferocious and deadly when the wind blows strongly over the swift tides. It's a popular place for contemplation and meditation.*

The 7-metre-tall obelisk was built by the lighthouse authority, Trinity House, as a navigational warning in 1844, well before the current 41-metre-high light was completed in 1906. There is now an interesting visitor centre in the former lighthouse-keepers' cottage.

A racing boat thunders past Pulpit Rock at close to 100mph during the spectacular annual Cowes-Torquay-Cowes powerboat race.

Opposite page: *The Bill from the south-west on a beautiful day. To the far left is Pulpit Rock.*
Inset: *Coasteerers near Wallsend.*

Evening gulls off Mutton Cove. In the distance is mighty Blacknor, once the site of a Victorian fort guarding the western side of Portland.

Opposite page: *Chesil Cove on a summer's evening. School students relax on the beach beneath the cottages of Chiswell village after completing their exams.*

Portland Harbour is productive for the local pot boats. *Inset: Portland Harbour has been strategically important for centuries and Henry VIII built two castles to defend it. Sandsfoot Castle to the north, completed in 1542 is, like the rest of the Jurassic Coast, continually subject to erosion and is slipping into the sea. It was held in turn by both Parliamentarians and Royalists during the English Civil War.*

Opposite: Portland Castle has survived superbly intact due to its well-sheltered position on the harbour's south bank.

5 Portland Harbour

PORTLAND HARBOUR ENCOMPASSES such a big chunk of the waters of the Jurassic Coast that I think it deserves a short chapter of its own.

It has an individual character with the vast breakwaters safely embracing its many and varied users like a loving mother's arms.

The Chesil Bank had always provided a refuge from the prevailing westerly winds and weather and the bay's shelter and strategic position were recognised by the military long before the breakwaters were built. Henry VIII installed two heavily-fortified castles to protect Portland Roads and his rapidly-expanding naval fleet.

The huge arms of Portland stone were added to provide more shelter for the nineteenth-century Royal Navy fleet and to protect the naval base from attack. When it was finally completed in 1872 – having used nearly six million tonnes of stone hewn from the island – it was the largest man-made harbour in the world and still occupies third position in that league. The breakwaters boast a total length of almost 3 miles and their construction was the most expensive public project in the country at that time.

The nearby Verne Prison was built to accommodate the prisoners whose labour was used to build the breakwaters.

The massive, circular, rusting Chequered Fort is one of only four iron-clad forts built along the south coast and has housed a variety of heavy guns over the years.

The Royal Navy left its dockyard in 1996 and Portland Port is now a flourishing commercial shipping enterprise and, in recent years, has become a busy and successful cruise ship port of call. The harbour also plays host to a range of water sports, from kite-surfing to scuba diving and is the centre for some of the finest sailing waters in Europe; indeed it was the host for the sailing events of the 2012 Olympic Games.

The lights of Underhill, Portland Port and the marina are reflected in the harbour waters at night.

Opposite page: *The sheltered harbour is continually in use as a sailing venue for events from small club series up to world-class regattas. Evening sunlight illuminates the sails of local dinghies in front of the buildings of Wyke Regis on the northern side of the harbour. Visible on the skyline are the TV relay transmitter and All Saints' church tower.*

Opposite page: *The sail training ship* Royalist, *alongside at Portland Marina, puts me in mind of a Turner painting ...*

Above: *Also in the multi-faceted marina, a family of peregrines squabble over a meal and, below, the former resident dolphin, Danny, plays with a kayaker.*

Portland Harbour was the home of the Royal Navy Air Station HMS Osprey for an amazing eighty-two years. After it formally closed in 1999 the area was renamed Osprey Quay and developed into the Weymouth and Portland National Sailing Academy and a new marina.

The base was a major training establishment for Royal Navy Lynx helicopters for many years and in 2017 there was a Lynx flypast to honour the role HMS Osprey played in the aircraft's huge success. It is pictured here flying over the former operations centre and air traffic control tower and one of the former Navy personnel accommodation blocks.

The village of Castletown was once the busy haunt of matelots from the Royal Navy dockyard. Some time after the Navy left, the area is now being redeveloped to include new homes, a museum and a diving centre, plus businesses associated with Portland Port.

Nevertheless, one of the huge former Navy accommodation blocks that dominate the skyline still awaits development and has become a somewhat notorious landmark.

Portland Port is now a thriving commercial enterprise and has brought huge benefits to the area since the Navy left. A large amount of shipping uses the deep-water port including an increasing number of cruise ships. The visiting cruise ship Norwegian Jade *is seen being refuelled by another local enterprise, Portland Bunkers UK Ltd.*

*   The port benefits from very clean water and schools of mullet are just one of the many species of wildlife that thrive in these industrial surroundings.*

In 2017, the Disney Magic, *pictured here passing the Chequered Fort, became the largest cruise ship ever to visit, at more than 1000 feet in length.*

Opposite page: *Portland Harbour covers around 1300 acres and the total length of the four breakwaters surrounding it is approaching 3 miles. At its widest the harbour is more than 2½ miles across.*

A flock of common scoter are seen at low level passing the mighty Chequered Fort. The fort's nickname (properly Fort Head) comes from the black and white squares that can be seen.

A sunray picks out the Moonfleet Manor Hotel behind the Chesil Beach.
The hamlet of Moonfleet was immortalised in J. Mead Falkner's eponymous
novel of smuggling and adventure which contains references to many local
spots. Of course the weather isn't always kind. Opposite is a trawler
working off Moonfleet Manor in some grimmer conditions.

6 The Mighty Chesil

THE CONSTANTLY SHIFTING Chesil Beach is one of the longest continuous barrier beaches in the world. From its south-eastern end at Chesil Cove on Portland to West Bay, near Bridport, where it meets the River Brit exiting West Bay Harbour, is about 18 miles. It averages 160 metres wide and around 12 metres high. I once read that it comprises about 180 billion pebbles, though it didn't say who counted them!

There is much expert debate about how the beach was created. One view is that the Chesil Beach initially formed from sandy deposits in Lyme Bay as water levels rose at the end of the last ice age 14,000 to 20,000 years ago. This sand and gravel was driven onshore to form a barrier beach and, by around 5000 years ago as sea levels stabilised, the bank was close to its current position.

At around this time erosion following the rise of the sea levels caused the cliffs of East Devon, the Budleigh pebble beds, to release huge quantities of gravel which was transported eastwards to the Chesil by a sea process called longshore drift. But there's still plenty of lively debate about it all.

Interestingly, the pebbles at the Portland end are much larger than at the Bridport end, due to tidal action and the action of longshore drift. It is said that in centuries past, fishermen landing on the beach in heavy fog could accurately tell where they were by the size of the pebbles.

Tucked behind the beach is the tidal, 8-mile long, Fleet Lagoon, which boasts the greatest variety of wildlife of any lagoon in the UK and which is also the largest in England.

A colony of little terns, one of the UK's rarest breeding seabirds, arrive from West Africa each spring to nest near the Portland end of the beach and Lyme Bay as a whole boasts an astonishing variety of wildlife. There are regular sightings of dolphins, porpoises, whales, sunfish and storm petrels to name just a few.

The beach changes hue according to the time of day, season and weather, from dazzling white to yellow, deep orange and brown ochres, and the continuity of the tone is broken by brightly-coloured anglers' brollies and windbreaks and assorted flotsam like red, blue and yellow pot buoys and fishermen's floats. I love the way rays of sunlight sometimes poke through the clouds like mother nature's spotlight following me along the Chesil.

At the western end lies the small resort of West Bay – known to millions of television fans as Broadchurch – alongside the striking flat-topped sandstone of West Cliff and Burton Cliff.

Below and opposite: Harvesting the land and the sea. The 18-mile coastal area of the Chesil Beach provides plenty for we humans. I wonder if the tractor drivers or trawler skippers ever get bored with the views from their office windows!

Dragon's Teeth and St Catherine's Chapel near Abbotsbury. During the Second World War the Chesil Beach was considered a prime location for possible enemy landings and was watched carefully along its entire length. There are many pillboxes both on the bank itself and in the fields beyond. At Abbotsbury there's still a barrier of 'Dragon's Teeth', concrete blocks designed to stop the lateral travel of enemy tanks and machinery should they ever be able to land on the bank.

It's interesting that St Catherine's Chapel, on the hill behind, seems to have remained standing in better condition, despite being nearly six centuries older!

Anglers and their brollies and windbreaks provide bright splashes of colour along most of the Chesil. Here at Abottsbury, they are backed by an old wall shielding some interesting and colourful flora atop Bullers Cliff. This patch of land is all that's left of the once-imposing house called Strangways (and later Abbotsbury Castle). It was built in the Gothic style in 1765 by the Countess of Ilchester, rebuilt after a major fire in 1913 and finally demolished in 1934. Although long-gone, its legacy is the extensive gardens which developed into the world-famous Abbotsbury Subtropical Gardens.

A pair of swans fly past the seaside village of West Bexington on their way to the swannery at Abbotsbury. Some of the beach huts in the background are sold for sums approaching a mind-boggling £300,000!

Late afternoon sunlight on the low mudstone cliffs near Burton Bradstock.

Right: *Hive Beach at Burton Bradstock. The two seaside villas atop Burton Cliff –
Barton Olivers and the Seaside Boarding House – were originally built as holiday
homes for a wealthy family in the late nineteenth century. In the distance is the
striking outline of Colmers Hill near Bridport, a popular subject with local artists.*

The western end of Burton Cliff.
The morning sun gives the sandstone a golden
glow which is reflected in the water.

90

The cliffs are constantly eroding and it's dangerous to walk too close to them. Falls like this one can occur without any warning...

Left: *A yacht sails along, from left, East, Freshwater and Burton Cliffs. The striking, flat-topped East Cliff became more iconic as the backdrop for the hugely-popular TV drama series* Broadchurch *which was set here.*

Right: *Until 2017 the Coastguard search and rescue helicopter based at Portland included the entire Jurassic Coast in its operational area and helped save many lives. Sadly, cost-cutting resulted in the end of this service.*

A fishing boat returns to West Bay Harbour with the peaks of Thorncombe Beacon, Doghouse Hill and Golden Cap as a backdrop.

7 The Heights of West Dorset

DEEP INTO WEST DORSET lie the highest and most physically-active stretches of the Jurassic Coast. From West Bay a line of towering cliffs and hills stretch out towards Lyme Regis and tallest of all is the majestic Golden Cap which, at 191 metres, also bears the honour of being the highest point on the south coast of England.

All the cliffs possess their own prosaic names: West Cliff, Fault Corner, Thorncombe Beacon, Doghouse Hill, Ridge Cliff, Stonebarrow...

Amongst the undulating hills lie the hamlets of Eypes Mouth, Seatown and the larger village of Charmouth, which vies with Lyme Regis as the fossil capital of England.

Overlooking Lyme Regis and separating it from Charmouth is the enigmatic and huge Black Ven, constantly changing and site of the largest mudslides in Europe. It is here that new material is constantly revealed by the shifting terraces – which are very obvious when viewed from seaward – making it one of the most productive fossil-hunting locations in the world and a major tourist attraction. Indeed, this is where the Lyme Regis born-and-bred godmother of palaeontology Mary Anning found her ichthyosaur skeleton in 1811.

The landslips vary in intensity from tiny rock showers to massive earth movements of thousands of tons. After heavy rain, water forms a perfect lubricant at the point where the bright greensands and chalk sit on top of the impermeable Jurassic clays. The former simply slide off the latter...

Golden Cap is a good example of this phenomenon and is so-called because of a layer of orange sandstone at the top which glows a deep gold in sunshine atop the darker clay and mudstone beneath.

A few hundred metres beyond The Cobb at pretty Lyme Regis, the county of Dorset comes to an end although, until the eighth century when West Saxon King Cynewulf granted a small parcel of land to the Bishopric of Sherborne in Dorset, the Cobb would have lain in Devon!

The Cobb itself has existed as a refuge and breakwater in one form or another since 1313. It was one of the first harbours constructed in Britain and is now Grade I listed.

The current structure is a massive, solid stone wall and protects the harbour, which was once a very significant trading post, from the prevailing south-westerly weather. It was built in the 1820s and the stone pier snakes its way out for 274 metres with thousands regularly enjoying a pleasant promenade along it in fine weather.

A warm summer day can set up huge cloud stacks which sometimes develop into thunderstorms. The size of these towering giants can be judged by noting Golden Cap, dwarfed at bottom centre of this image.

Opposite page: *The pretty seaside village of Eype, near Bridport. The popular beach boasts spectacular views along the West Dorset coast.*

Seatown is a hamlet near the village of Chideock. It lies at the mouth of the Wynreford stream and once had 30 or 40 fishermen who no doubt earned far more from the rife smuggling that went on here than from fishing... The popular Anchor Inn is busy year round.

The ubiquitous Red Arrows are regular visitors to events at Lyme Regis and are seen here climbing high over nearby Golden Cap during the town's Community Week.

Below: *Late afternoon sunlight on Golden Cap and Thorncombe Beacon. Seatown lies between the two.*

The village of Charmouth, between Black Ven and Stonebarrow at the mouth of the River Char, is a thriving holiday destination and a top UK location for fossil hunters. The surrounding cliffs teem with fossils and there are organised walks for hunters all year round. Winter is often the best time to visit as stormy weather erodes the cliffs and constantly releases new specimens. Many thousands of schoolchildren visit the village's Heritage Coast Centre every year on educational trips.

Opposite page, top: *The lonely beach at St Gabriel's Mouth, at the western base of Golden Cap, is backed by the woods of Langdon Hill.* Bottom: *Harvesting at Upcot Farm, near Morcombelake.*

Black Ven's colourful terraces can be striking when viewed from offshore.

Porous stone lets water through to the underlying clay which becomes very slippery after rain and the rock simply slides off in large chunks. Ammonites and belemnites are very common here along with fossilised fish and much larger reptiles.

Lyme Regis needs little introduction. Best viewed from offshore, the pretty town has been a favourite holiday destination for centuries, though it grew to prominence in the thirteenth century as a major port.
In 1644 the Parliamentarian townsfolk famously withstood an eight-week siege by Royalists.

Like many seaside towns in the south west, Lyme has a thriving and competitive gig rowing following and teams can be seen practising at most times of the year.

Left: *Lyme's legendary Cobb shelters the harbour and has featured in many novels and films. For the tens of thousands who visit every year, it's popular to stroll along the top of the massive stone wall, just like Meryl Streep in the movie of* The French Lieutenant's Woman. *In the distance, the greenery at the eastern end of the Underhill can be seen.*

105

Heading west out of Lyme gives a stunning view of the town from outside the Cobb. The town is backdropped by the terraced strata of Black Ven cliff, the site of one of Europe's largest active landslips.
Inset: *Fishing nets make a colourful sculpture on the quayside.*

Opposite page: *Midsummer dawn from the mooring pontoons at Lyme Regis. The pontoons have boosted the maritime economy of the town enabling visiting yachts to berth more securely and are erected and dismantled each season to avoid damage from any severe winter weather.*
    Looking over the side of the boat after dark sometimes reveals the water boiling with a myriad mackerel.

Huts at Monmouth Beach. The beach was so-named after the eponymous Duke landed here in 1685 at the start of the Monmouth Rebellion, the attempt to overthrow the newly-crowned James II.

Opposite page: *Seeing into Devon. Just to the west of Lyme Regis, looking steamy and primordial, the wild and unhospitable Undercliff covers some 5 miles of the 7 miles to Seaton, encompassing the border between Dorset and Devon.*

Shafts of sunlight beam down onto Devonshire waters. The headlands of Seven Rock Point, Culverhole and Beer Head are visible.

8 Into Devon

LYME REGIS LIES at the western edge of Dorset and is a matter of a few hundred metres from the Devon border which is where, coincidentally, the longest – the Jurassic – stretch of the World Heritage Site starts to give way to the older, red sandstones of Devon.

The coastal landscape for the 5 miles between Lyme and Axmouth is one of mostly wild and untamed jungle-type vegetation and is known as the Undercliff. Caused by centuries of landslips and tumbles, the area is difficult to access, with deep gullies and dense undergrowth, and forms a rare type of habitat for trees, plants, birds, animals and butterflies which thrive on the isolation. No one has lived here for more than a century.

The writer John Fowles described it as 'the nearest this country can offer to a tropical jungle'.

The stretch encompasses the Axmouth to Lyme Regis Undercliffs National Nature Reserve, one of the highlights of the Jurassic Coast and it certainly makes a challenging walk – with no access points along its length, you either have to turn back or carry on.

The biggest landslip here was at Christmas 1839 when a stretch of arable land about ¾ of a mile long, and estimated at 8 million tons, slipped and fell outwards forming a deep, half-mile-wide chasm behind. The land is known as Goat Island and is now a particularly good habitat for butterflies and orchids.

Interestingly, the arable land remained intact enough to be successfully harvested the following summer!

The first habitation reached when emerging from the Undercliff is the village of Axmouth at the eastern end of the resort of Seaton. Now a tiny harbour, it was once a major port until land movements and silting made it very difficult for vessels to access. Perhaps surprisingly, in the mid-fourteenth century it accounted for around a fifth of the entire country's shipping trade.

The popular Devon resort of Seaton is bordered to the west by the pretty village of Beer, a bustling fishing village where the few remaining boats are winched up onto the shingle beach after each day's work.

Stone has been worked from the nearby quarries since Roman times and the flint in layers in the surrounding chalk cliffs is thought to have been traded between 2000 and 4000BC.

To the west of the village, and sheltering it from the prevailing weather, are the steep cliffs of Beer Head, the most westerly chalk headland in the country. Another major landslide, the Hooken slip, took place here in 1790 when 10 acres of land slid perpendicularly down the headland. This has since become a wooded and sheltered habitat with chalk pinnacles on the seaward side.

Sunlight picks out Charton Bay in the Undercliff with Beer Head in the distance. The Lyme rowing gig Black Ven can be seen off Seven Rock Point.

Left: *The first bay into Devon, Pinhay, shows some of the last of the Jurassic strata heading west before the older, Triassic, sandstones start to dominate. Colourful falls line the back of the beach and in late summer, trees show a variety of shades as they climb into the Undercliff.*

Right: *Charton Bay from offshore. This part of the Undercliff is a major area of land movement and due to its difficult accessibility has become a haven for rare and unusual flora and fauna. The landslip plateau of Goat Island can be seen to the left, with Dowlands to the right.*

The Goat Island plateau was formed during the Dowlands landslip of Christmas 1839 when a section of rough pasture land slid downwards and forwards to leave a deep chasm behind thus creating the 'island'. Fortunately for us, geologists William Conybeare and William Buckland were surveying the area at the time and subsequently produced the first full scientific report of a major landslip. Their conclusions are still considered valid. For years after there was great national interest in the phenomenon and even Queen Victoria visited to view the sight from her yacht.

Rainbow cliffs near Axmouth at the western end of the Undercliff.

The entrance to pretty Axmouth Harbour at Seaton. Once one of the busiest ports in England, landslips and silting have meant access to the tiny harbour is now considered challenging. It is only used by leisure boaters and a handful of fishermen. The entrance dries completely at low tide and can just be seen in the centre of the picture. Devon's red Triassic sandstone is now becoming evident.

Right: The ubiquitous black-backed gulls – these look like they're in a stacking system awaiting landing instructions from air traffic control!

Axmouth Quay, with its colourful fishing boats, lies along the eastern side of the estuary. Seaton provided ships and men for Edward I's wars with Scotland and France, but a fourteenth-century storm caused a major landslip which largely blocked the estuary.

Opposite page: Red mudstone cliffs form the western end of the Seaton promenade with colourful beach huts at the bottom and a handsome white terrace at the top.

Heading west, Seaton is the first coastal town in East Devon. The popular resort developed in the eighteenth century and is a peaceful place with a shingle beach which has built up to the west of the Axe estuary.

Due to a geological fault, the red mudstone gives way to much younger Cretaceous chalk at White Cliff, approaching Beer, west of Seaton. This continues on the other side of the combe in which Beer sits.

Picture-postcard Beer, with its traditional flint cottages, is sheltered from the prevailing westerly winds and still boasts a small fleet of beach-launched fishing boats. It's surrounded by stunning walks and was named the top picnic spot in the UK by the BBC *Countryfile* show.

Beer boasts many claims to fame. It was once a major smuggling village and also produced the lace for the flounce of Queen Victoria's wedding dress. Stone mined from Beer quarry caves, prized since Roman times, was partly used to build St Paul's Cathedral and Westminster Abbey, and local crab and mackerel are said to be among the best in the west.

The promontory of Beer Head is the site of the great Hooken Landslide of 1790 when a 10-acre tract slumped and is now a wooded and sheltered habitat with striking pinnacles on the seaward side. The slip is clearly seen in this photograph. These chalk cliffs are the most westerly in England.

9 Desert Dust

FROM HERE ON THE dominant coastal colour is red. The legendary red Devon soil is Triassic sandstone, laid down more than 200 million years ago, before the Jurassic period, when the area was desert and we were sitting much nearer to the Equator in the single giant continent of Pangea.

This was of course a hot, dry and inhospitable climate and the fossils found here are mostly small, indicative of the creatures of a desert habitat.

Initially there are a few stretches of the red coast that have chalk sitting on top but it all soon gives way to red, and nothing but.

It's interesting how the much younger Cretaceous chalk got to lie directly atop the ancient Triassic sandstone when there were some 56 million years of the Jurassic period between them.

Looking past Beer Head it can be seen that the view is red. Mostly. Although the promontory is England's most westerly chalk headland, the white rock still makes a few further appearances directly atop the much older Triassic sandstone as we head towards Sidmouth. This apparent anomaly is one of the unusual features that makes this World Heritage Site unique.

It's intriguing how the hues can change from deep orange to salmon pink depending on the angle of view, the time of year and the position of the sun.

The reason, basically, is erosion. In very simple terms, (because that's all I understand), after the Triassic period came the Jurassic and then the Cretaceous. But during the 80-million-year Cretaceous came the 'big tilt' from massive uplifts due to tectonic plate movements. The western part of the coast was pushed up, causing a tilt downwards to the east.

That's why the Jurassic Coast is so unusual. Erosion wore the top off it all and left the periodic layers of rock alongside rather than on top of each other. But that's not quite the end of it – there were still millions of years of Cretaceous deposits to be laid down above.

After our old friend erosion did its job and took most of the top layer of chalk away, just a few humps remained which are where we see the white directly on top of the red here in East Devon.

Heading down towards Sidmouth means passing a rolling landscape of steep, wooded hills either side of valleys with pebble beaches, called mouths, the first of which is Branscombe Mouth.

The linear village of Branscombe became world famous in January 2007 when the large container ship MSC *Napoli* was deliberately grounded about a mile off the beach. She had developed a cracked hull and flooded engine room in a storm and the questionable decision was taken by the government's representative to beach her here to enable salvage work to take place. As the contents of the ship's containers began to wash up on the beach there were scenes of frantic scavenging by some people which ended up being ignominiously broadcast on news reports across the world.

The next flat-topped hills, between 400 and 500 feet high, show chalk sitting on top of sandstone. Colourful Berry Cliff, Dunscombe Cliff and verdant Salcombe Hill are separated by the valleys of Weston Mouth and Salcombe Mouth.

The coastal town of bustling Sidmouth sits next to High Peak hill which presents a steep and eroded red face before we reach the striking Triassic sandstone stacks of Ladram Bay, reminiscent of the larger chalk ones at Old Harry Rocks.

Rounding the next headland, Otterton Point, the stately resort of Budleigh Salterton is revealed, nestled between the picturesque River Otter estuary and more blushing sandstone cliffs. It's thought that a huge ancient river used to flow northwards from Brittany through here that deposited many of the pebbles that eventually helped to form the Chesil Beach further to the east.

There's a 2-mile shingle beach backed by high cliffs before the low, flat headland of the prosaically-named Straight Point is reached, which separates Budleigh from Exmouth. Apparently, there is a bylaw which restricts the removal of pebbles from Budleigh beach, enforced by a fine of £2000 per pebble!

Straight Point has a live firing range on the top used by Marines from the nearby training centre at Lympstone.

Opposite page: *Put very simply, Jurassic limestones would originally have been laid down on top of the Triassic sandstone. Earth movements during the early Cretaceous period caused a huge tilt to the east, and erosion subsequently wore down these layers until the later Cretaceous greensands and chalk were laid down directly on top. Hence, white on red instead of white on blue on red!*

The result can be seen in this image of Berry and Dunscombe Cliffs. (Sidmouth can be seen at extreme left.)

Round the corner from Beer Head lies Branscombe beach with the now-verdant Hooken Cliffs towering above. Clinging to the edge are a collection of delightfully-situated holiday chalets which must be a wonderful choice for a tranquil break.

Shingle now continues at the waterline almost continuously to Sidmouth with some attractive, though challenging, spots for a day visit or picnic.

Rising above the back of the beaches are the imposing red sandstone Berry Cliff, Dunscombe Cliff and Salcombe Hill, separated by the ends of valleys called 'mouths'. This image shows the steep hike to and from Weston Mouth, situated in a geological fault between Berry and Dunscombe Cliffs.

Dunscombe Cliff clearly shows the Cretaceous greensands and chalk sittting high above Triassic sandstone. A large slide can be seen to the left.

Verdant Salcombe Mouth and its beach sit between the flat-topped Dunscombe Cliff and Salcombe Hill (named from the nearby village of Salcombe Regis, not the South Devon harbour).

A large part of elegant Sidmouth has been designated a conservation area and it's easy to see why from seaward. Originally a fishing village, the town developed when the fashion for coastal resorts in Georgian and Victorian times took off and many Regency and Georgian buildings line the handsome seafront.

A harbour has never been completed at Sidmouth, largely due to its direct exposure to the prevailing south-westerly weather, and protective rock islands or groynes have now been built to shelter the seafront and esplanade after continual erosion, above.

In 1819, Edward, Duke of Kent, his wife and baby daughter spent several weeks in Woodbrook Glen (now a hotel) in the town, where Edward sadly died from an illness. The baby grew up to be Queen Victoria.

Above and opposite page: *Leaving Sidmouth astern takes us past towering Peak Hill and the approach to stunning Ladram Bay. The shallow bay boasts impressive red sandstone stacks, not dissimilar to those white ones at Old Harry Rocks at the other end of the Jurassic Coast, although perhaps 150 million years separate them.*

The sandstone and mudstone were laid down more than 200 million years ago in the Triassic period when the region sat much nearer to the equator – within the Pangea super-continent – and was desert.

In some areas colourful greenery clings to the cliff face while most of the bay fronts a glowing red backdrop.

A pair of white-beaked dolphins are pictured with Ladram Bay in the distance.

Heading out of Ladram Bay will take us westwards round Otterton Point.

Opposite page, top: *Otterton Point features an extensive ledge which can be very turbulent in bad conditions and is given a wide berth by mariners. The River Otter flows into the sea here and separates the point from the seaside town of Budleigh Salterton.* Bottom: *The ledges are a productive spot for fishermen and, of course, the local gulls!*

Beautiful Budleigh Salterton is the epitome of a traditional seaside town with attractive period buildings and a 2-mile long beach. The pebbles that make up the beach were carried here by an ancient river, from what is now Brittany, during the Triassic period and, due to various processes, millions of these are to be found in beaches further east and in the Chesil Beach back in Dorset.

The green-topped red cliffs of Budleigh Bay continue as far as Straight Point, the last headland in the Jurassic Coast journey west.

The prosaically-named Straight Point marks the western boundary of Budleigh's beautiful bay, and the start of the run into Exmouth.

Used for rifle practise by soldiers from the Royal Marines' training base at nearby Lympstone, one of the range safety lookout points can be seen to the right.

10 The West End

ALTHOUGH THE SANDSTONE continues for many more miles through Devon, the section included in the Jurassic Coast World Heritage Site ends with the Geoneedle monument – unveiled by Prince Charles in 2002 after World Heritage status was granted – at Orcombe Point, just outside Exmouth.

So, just as the far eastern end of the Jurassic Coast is bounded by a popular coastal town, so the western end is marked by the beautiful resort of Exmouth, facing the Jurassic Coast to its east.

The town is a port and busy seaside resort which really became established in the eighteenth century. It's considered the oldest resort in Devon and grew popular as a destination for the wealthy to improve their health, although most of the town was built during the Victorian era with the arrival of the railway and mass tourism.

The town docks is now a handsome and colourful marina development and the town's frontage, behind the long, sandy beach is handsome indeed.

Sitting alongside the River Exe estuary, this is where the district of East Devon ends and that of Teignbridge begins.

Opposite page: *Straight Point hosts a large colony of cormorants whose 'guano' provides a bright, if unappettising, contrast to the prevailing sandstone.*

Right: *A yacht passes the rising cliff toward Orcombe Point.*

Behind Straight Point, and near the far western end of the Jurassic Coast, lies Sandy Bay and the large holiday park of Devon Cliffs.

The sediments here form the oldest part of the coast, at around 250 million years, as well as providing a safe, attractive beach.

Traditionally, most people would never have experienced the beauty of this part of the world and in days gone by this coastline was the exclusive haunt of wealthy Victorian tourists. But with the advent of cheap transport and the concept of the 'annual holiday' the coastline was opened up to all and, while many decry the positioning of holiday parks along the coast, they seem to contribute to a pragmatic, if inelegant, move to a more egalitarian society.

At the western end of Sandy Bay the cliffs rise again to Orcombe Point and the official western boundary of the Jurassic Coast.

When the coast was awarded World Heritage status in 2002, the inauguration was celebrated with the unveiling by Prince Charles of a stone monument called a geoneedle. The angular monument was sculpted by Michael Fairfax from a variety of rocks laid in the sequence of those of the Jurassic Coast.

At the south-eastern end of Exmouth the old gently-rising cliff line can be seen with hotels atop, behind the former extended beach area which is now built upon with an attractive promenade, road and gardens.

This part of the town forms the western end of the exposure of the Triassic cliffs which constitute such a long and striking part of the Jurassic Coast.

Exmouth's regal and colourful seafront forms a handsome western bookend to the Jurassic Coast World Heritage Site.

The images in this book can be purchased by visiting www.stevebelasco.net